STRANGE AND SCARY CREATURES

INVESTIGATING HISTORY'S MYSTERIES

Louise Spilsbury

CHERITON
CHILDREN'S BOOKS

Published in 2024 by **Cheriton Children's Books**
1 Bank Drive West, Shrewsbury, Shropshire, SY3 9DJ, UK

© 2024 Cheriton Children's Books

First Edition

Author: Louise Spilsbury
Designer: Jessica Moon
Editor: Jennifer Sanderson
Proofreader: Ella Hammond

Picture credits: Cover: Shutterstock/Daniel Eskridge. Inside: p1: Shutterstock/Warpaint, p4: Shutterstock/JM_Media, p5: Shutterstock/Fer Gregory, p7l: Shutterstock/Warpaint, p7r: Shutterstock/Chaiyapruek Youprasert, p8: Shutterstock/Kolbakova Olga, p9l: Shutterstock/Rudmer Zwerver, p9r: Shutterstock/Bragapictures, p10: Shutterstock/Sport08, p11: Shutterstock/Roman Mikhailiuk, p12: Shutterstock/Daniel Eskridge, p13: Shutterstock/Taras Stelmah, p15: Shutterstock/GrandeDuc, p17: Shutterstock/Digital Storm, p18: Shutterstock/Rbrown10, p19: Shutterstock/Rudall30, p20: Shutterstock/Daniel Eskridge, p23: Shutterstock/RikoBest, p24: Shutterstock/Iobard, p25: Shutterstock/Daniel Eskridge, p27: Shutterstock/Daniel Eskridge, p29l: Shutterstock/Solarseven, p29r: Shutterstock/Andrea Izzotti, p30: Shutterstock/Warpaint, p31: Shutterstock/Daniel Eskridge, p32: Shutterstock/Warpaint, p34l: Shutterstock/Warpaint, p34r: Shutterstock/Mark Brandon, p35: Shutterstock/Funstarts33, p37: Shutterstock/Melnikov Dmitriy, p38: Shutterstock/Mysikrysa, p39: Wikimedia Commons/Daderot, p40: Wikimedia Commons/Martin Lewison, p41: Shutterstock/IG Digital Arts, p42: Shutterstock/Danny Ye, p43: Shutterstock/Dariush M, p45b: Wikimedia Commons/Helena.40proof, p45t: Shutterstock/Marcin Sylwia Ciesielski.

Printed in China

Please visit our website,
www.cheritonchildrensbooks.com
to see more of our high-quality books.

CONTENTS

CHAPTER 1

NOISES IN THE NIGHT

There's a full moon in the sky but dark, heavy clouds bring a spooky gloom to the night. A chill fills the air. There's an eerie howling sound nearby and whispering in the shadows... The idea that something or someone is out there in the dark, perhaps waiting to do us harm, has always frightened people. But, are there strange and scary creatures out there? Or is there a simpler explanation for the noises we might hear in the night?

Creatures Find a Home

Scary creatures vary around the world, depending on the type of place they come from. For example, a hunter-gatherer community relies on hunting wild animals for food. These people may tell stories of beasts that are connected to hunting and the chase. A farming community usually fears monsters who live or wait on the edge of their village or near the fields. People living near forests often fear beasts that may lurk among the trees.

Trick or Treat?

Many people love to dress as scary creatures for Halloween but would they enjoy it so much if they knew the spooky stories behind these monsters? Take the Grim Reaper as an example. This eerie figure represents death. It looks like a skeleton cloaked in a black robe and carries a farming tool called a scythe, which is used to cut down crops. The reaper carries this because it is said to **harvest** human souls from the earth.

The Jersey Devil is said to be a demon that stalks dark forests in the Pine Barrens of New Jersey.

The Grim Reaper in its sinister-looking black robes appears suddenly, without making a sound.

The Grim Reaper in its sinister-looking black robes appears suddenly, without making a sound.

The Reaper Is Grim!

Legends say that when the Grim Reaper appears, it is a sign someone will die. When the last grain of sand falls in the hourglass the Reaper holds, it collects the soul of its victim with a single swing of its scythe. The idea of the Grim Reaper originated, or started, in the fourteenth century during the time of the Black Death. The Black Death was the name for a terrible disease called Bubonic Plague, which swept through Europe and killed millions of people. It turned its victims' fingers and toes black before they died. No wonder terrified people began to talk of a Grim Reaper.

SET TO SPOOK!

In this book, we are going to explore some of the most mystifying and unsettling reports about strange and scary creatures—reports that have been made by ordinary people, scientists, authors, and doctors. Some of the stories will send shivers down your spine. Some of them will leave you truly spooked!

Meet the Zombies

Zombies are beasts that come back from the dead to cause terror in the living world. Their only thought is to attack and feed on the flesh of living humans. They never get tired and they will not stop until they get what they want. Zombies have no feelings and show no mercy to their victims. Legend has it that there are only two ways to stop a zombie: destroy its brain or cut off its head! After a person has been bitten by a zombie, they become a zombie too.

Making Myths

The stories of zombies came from seventeenth-century Haiti in Central America. It was said that a bokor, or a **voodoo** priest, could turn a living person into a zombie by putting two special powders into a wound on their body. Using a poison found in pufferfish, called tetrodotoxin, can almost kill a person. This poison was then mixed with a second powder that could put the person in a trance-like state where they did exactly as they were told.

Back from the Dead

Deep in the dark tombs beneath ancient Egyptian pyramids, the **archeologists** who went there must have felt cold, breathed musty air, and been scared of the strange shadows made by their flickering lanterns. Creaking open the dusty coffin inside, it must have been eerie to find a dead **pharaoh** wrapped in faded bandages: a mummy! And next to the mummy, there was likely a curse written on the tomb wall.

A Mummy's Curse

Not long after discoveries of Egyptian mummies and curses on tomb walls hit the world's headlines, stories of spine-tingling deaths followed. There were reports of those who visited the tombs dying unexpectedly. The idea of pharaohs returning from the dead to take revenge on anyone who had disturbed their tombs haunted people.

SPOOKED!

Egyptians believed that making mummies prepared people for the **afterlife**. After a body was cleaned, its brain and other **internal organs** were removed. The body was covered in a type of salt to dry it out and oiled to stop the skin cracking. The body was stuffed to give it shape and then wrapped in strips of linen cloth. The mummy was then sealed inside two coffins with objects for it to use in the next world.

It was said that angry mummies would return to torment people who had entered their tombs!

Zombies are terrifying creatures that rise up from their graves.

BLOOD SUCKERS

Frightening Fangs

Vampires are very much the creatures of nightmares. These monsters leave their graves at night to feast on human blood. They drain their victims' blood using their snakelike teeth, or fangs. This kills their prey and turns it into a vampire, too. Apart from their long, white fangs and eerily pale, white skin, vampires look spookily like humans in almost every other way.

Spot and Stop

It is said that vampires mostly hunt at night because sunlight weakens their powers and burns their skin. That's why they often attack victims who are asleep in their beds. Vampires are incredibly strong and can **hypnotize** their victims, so they also attack people who are awake. Some vampires can even change into a bat or a wolf. They cannot see their reflection in a mirror and cast no shadows. In some stories, they also rise in the day if there are heavy mists or dark clouds. Vampires can only be stopped by crosses, silver, and garlic. To end a vampire's reign of terror, they must be stabbed in the heart with a wooden **stake**. Some say it is safest to cut off the creature's head, too!

Legends say that vampires are scary, blood-drinking creatures of the night.

Some old skeletons from Eastern Europe have been found with their teeth removed and signs that they were stabbed through the heart with a rod.

Death and Disease

Fears of vampires were widespread in the **Middle Ages**. At this time, the Bubonic Plague wiped out entire towns. Some people think that vampire legends could have come from a lack of understanding about how diseases spread. Fearful about why people were dying in such large numbers, people looked for other reasons to explain the deaths.

Vampires Among Them

People imagined vampires were living among them and that they were the cause of the deaths. The Plague could cause mouth sores that would bleed, which some took to be a sign of being a vampire. Another disease that could have affected people at that time causes nasty blisters to form on the skin in sunlight, and this may have led to the idea that vampires hated the Sun.

Taking Control

Vampires were a very real fear in Europe for hundreds of years. Trying to kill vampires or stop them from feeding was a way for people to try to control whatever was killing their friends and families. They devised grim **rituals** to perform on dead bodies to stop them becoming vampires.

CHAPTER 2

A WORLD OF BEASTS

Many of the scary creatures found in mythical tales were created long ago to explain things people didn't understand. Some of these beasts were simply evil but others were dreamed up to serve as a lesson, telling people how to behave or serving as warnings about real dangers. It's unlikely any of them were ever real, although there are those who may still believe in them.

Gruesome Goblins

The small and ugly goblins from **folk tales** in the United Kingdom (UK) are mean and mischievous creatures. Strange and creepy goblins in Cornwall, England, are known as spriggans. They look like small, scary old men with oversized heads. Spriggans cause storms to frighten travelers and ruin crops. They also steal babies. Knockers are goblins that live in mines where they cause mining accidents and rockslides. They likely came from miners' tales about knocking and tapping sounds heard while working in the deep dark.

The Spider Teacher

Anansi is a legendary creature that is famous throughout Africa, the Caribbean, and beyond. Anansi can shape-shift, or change form, but usually looks like a spider with a human head. Anansi is known as a trickster—a figure that is sneaky and sly. It uses its cunning wit to outsmart those around it to get what it wants, even if that causes problems for the humans it meets. However, Anansi also teaches people important lessons, often through challenges and puzzles.

Goblins are ugly and scary creatures.

Were some spooky legends created to stop children exploring old mines and other unsafe places?

Lessons with Anansi

There are many stories about Anansi. In one tale, Anansi is said to have gathered all of the world's knowledge and stored it in a **gourd** because it did not trust humans with so much information. It soon realized that however hard it tried, scraps of knowledge kept spilling out of the gourd. This taught it, and us, that it was not right for one person to try to know everything and to hold it for themself. It is better for knowledge to be shared among everyone.

SPOOKED!

In Scotland, there are tales of a goblin named Redcap who dyes its hat with human blood!

11

Watch Out for the Wendigo!

The wendigo is a terrifying character found in the myths of some North American tribes. Legends say that the first sign you are being followed by a monstrous wendigo is a foul stench, or smell. The wendigo smells of rotten meat because it has an uncontrollable appetite for human flesh. This fearsome beast may have sunken or glowing eyes, sharp fangs and claws, pointed ears, and horns or antlers like a deer. A wendigo can only be destroyed by silver, steel, or iron bullets, a dagger, or by having its heart burned in a fire.

Why Wendigos?

Winters were long and harsh in the cold woodlands of Canada and northern parts of the United States, and food would have been scarce. Some people believe that wendigos represent cold and hunger, and that stories about these beasts were intended to be a reminder to people about the need to work together and share things to survive such times, rather than be greedy and selfish.

Some people think the legend of the wendigo may have come from real-life cases of people who were so hungry in icy winters that they ate other members of their tribe.

The wendigo legend also acted as a warning to children not to stray far into the woods.

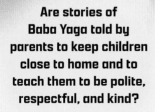

Baba Yaga

Baba Yaga is an ogress, or female ogre, from Eastern European folk tales. Her name translates very roughly to "wicked old woman" and stories of this larger-than-life character have terrified children for centuries. Baba Yaga is said to live in a hut deep within dark forests. This hut is propped up on chicken legs and is constantly spinning. The fence around it is made of human bones and topped with human skulls. Baba Yaga sometimes flies around in a giant iron **mortar** that she drives with a **pestle**, whipping up storms as she goes. She is said to kidnap her victims, usually children, and then cook them on her enormous stove, before eating them.

Lessons for Life

Some people say that spooky characters like Baba Yaga were created to teach children valuable life lessons. Stories of Baba Yaga suggest that if children talk to her with respect, she lets them go. If they are rude or they don't follow rules and get lost in the forest, she will capture and eat them. Parents still sometimes use Baba Yaga's name to stop children from wandering far from home.

Are stories of Baba Yaga told by parents to keep children close to home and to teach them to be polite, respectful, and kind?

The Worm of Death

The Mongolian death worm is a scary creature people claim lives below the sands in the Gobi Desert in Mongolia, Asia. The death worm has never been photographed but witnesses describe it as a long, thick worm, with blood-red skin that is 5 feet (1.5 m) long. It has spikes that stick out of both ends of its body. It is called a death worm because it kills victims in fearsome ways. It can spit a deadly stream of venom, or poison, and it can also produce electric shocks powerful enough to kill an adult human.

Is It Real?

Some people say witnesses have mistaken either a worm lizard, which can be big and burrows, or digs, underground, or a sand boa snake for the legendary death worm. However, there are worms that can live in sand instead of soil, like the giant beach worm in Australia. So, could it be real? The Gobi Desert is an enormous region that spans a territory of 500,000 square miles (1,300,000 square km) of wild, **remote** land, so it is possible that there are undiscovered animals in it.

The Beastly Basilisk

Another creature that is said to kill using deadly venom is the basilisk. The basilisk is a monster that struck fear into people's hearts for centuries across Europe and North Africa. This strange, mythical creature is often pictured as a combination of a reptile and rooster, with the head, feathers, and front legs of a rooster, and a reptile's tail and scaly wings.

A Death Stare

The basilisk is perhaps the most feared of all mythical beasts because it could also destroy any animal or plant simply by looking at it or breathing on it. Some say it can shatter stones with its deadly breath too. The basilisk's venom is said to be so powerful, that if it drank from a well, the water was polluted for centuries, and would kill anyone who drank it too.

SPOOKED!

According to legend, basilisks can only be stopped in a few ways. The sound of a rooster crowing or the odor, or smell, of a weasel can destroy it. Or it can destroy itself with its death stare if you hold a mirror up to its face.

The dreaded Mongolian death worm has inspired movies and illustrations, like this one.

INVESTIGATING
TERRIFYING TROLLS

Strong and Ugly

Mysterious rock formations with strange troll-like shapes have intrigued people in Norway, Iceland, and other parts of **Scandinavia** for centuries. Trolls are legendary monsters that came out only at night, in the dark. If they don't get back to their hiding places before the morning, the first rays of sunlight turn them into stone. Trolls are said to be very strong, very ugly, and have a taste for humans.

Types of Trolls

Some trolls can be gigantic and **sinister**, while others can be small and playful. Trolls of the mountain and of the forest are generally shown as big, cruel creatures. They are said to uproot trees to use as clubs for hitting people, and to be able to cause hurricanes and avalanches. Cave trolls live completely underground. They are often pictured as smaller than humans, with a large round belly, short arms and legs, and slimy skin. One theory about trolls is that they were invented long ago as a way to frighten children so that they wouldn't go out after dark.

Troll Troubles

Trolls are thought to have been around for centuries. There's no evidence, or proof, that they ever actually existed but in legends, most trolls are dangerous to people. They set **riddles** that people must solve if they are to be allowed to escape. Some trolls are thieves, entering homes under a cloak of invisibility to steal food and cause other mischief. The worst trolls were said to eat humans and farm animals, which they captured and ran off with during night raids.

Outwitting a Troll

All trolls have some things in common. As well as being unfriendly to humans, they're also usually so stupid that people can outwit them. One tale tells of a boy who met an angry troll when he went into the deep forest to fetch wood. Luckily, the boy had taken a piece of cheese with him for a snack. He pulled the cheese out of his pocket and pretended it was a rock. To fool the troll into thinking he had great strength, the boy squeezed the cheese "rock" until the **whey** came out. The troll was terrified and offered to help the boy chop wood to keep him happy!

Some trolls are said
to live under bridges,
where they lie in wait
for passing prey to eat!

CHAPTER 3

HAIRY HORRORS

Scary creatures covered in hair feature in many legends across the world. Many look strangely like animals we recognize but with small, spooky differences. It is unsettling to hear or see creatures that might be monsters, but could they simply be wolves, bears, or other animals? The fact is that some legendary monsters do, amazingly, turn out to be real.

New Discoveries

Some of the animals we know are real today were once thought to be imaginary. The curious striped okapi resembles a horse, a giraffe, and a zebra and it is a very shy animal. It was talked about for years by local people in the Congo in Africa but only recorded by scientists in 1902. Scientists discover new **species** every year. In 2023, for example, a new species of hairy hedgehog was discovered in mountains in the Philippines.

SPOOKED!

The mountain gorilla was believed to be a mythical beast until a German Army officer named Friedrich Robert von Beringe shot two of the animals.

The mountain gorilla species was officially named *Gorilla beringei* after the man who proved their existence.

Belief in werewolves is found throughout the world and throughout history.

Wolves of the Full Moon

Werewolves are said to be humans who turn into large, vicious wolflike monsters during each full moon. They turn back into human form when daylight comes. While the person is in their werewolf form, they have an uncontrollable urge to eat human flesh. Once they bite a victim, that person is cursed too and will become a werewolf themself at the next full moon. People who are unlucky enough to suffer the curse of the werewolf do not want to change into a beast but they are powerless to stop it.

Werewolf Legends

Some people say that there are explanations for the werewolf legend. Stories of werewolves in North America may be linked to Native Americans who wore animal skins while hunting, and possibly to scare other tribes. In 1725, a boy was found wandering naked on all fours through a German forest. It is thought that wolves may have raised the boy. He ate with his hands and couldn't speak. Many thought he was a werewolf. Some diseases could also result in behaviors that spark such fears. Rabies, for example, is a disease dogs can get. If transferred to humans, it can cause them to behave strangely, to foam at the mouth, and be more aggressive.

The rougarou is said to be on the look-out for misbehaving children!

Swamp Monsters

At night in the swamps of central and eastern Louisiana, fog often hangs low on the muddy ground, and the sounds of animals moving in the dark fills the air. This is the home of the legendary rougarou, a towering beast with the body of a man and the head of a wolf or dog. It is covered in black hair. Like the werewolf, the rougarou is supposed to be a human who has been cursed. This terrifying monster has sharp teeth and claws, and prowls around the swamps, attacking or cursing anyone it sees.

Running with the Rougarou

The stories of the rougarou were most likely inspired by tales from France of werewolves called loup-garou. People brought these stories with them when they moved to Canada and the southern United States in the eighteenth century. Many people think stories about the rougarou were used to scare children into behaving. However, some believe there are footprints and even a video to prove that the monster exists, and there have even been alleged sightings in recent years.

A Goat Killer?

The chupacabra is a fanged beast with red, glowing eyes that attacks livestock and sucks their blood. The name chupacabra comes from Spanish words meaning "goat sucker." The first rumors of this vicious, hairy beast appeared in Puerto Rico in the 1990s, when goats and chickens died in unusual circumstances with their blood completely drained. Stories of the chupacabra spread through Mexico and the United States, where deaths of livestock also occurred.

Chupacabra or Coyote?

The chupacabra is a large, heavy creature with big fangs and claws, and a backbone covered with sharp spines. Some say it looks a little like a human or ape, and walks on two legs or hops like a kangaroo. Others say that it crawls along on all fours. Some people claim to have seen dead chupacabra but scientists say those animals were probably coyotes that had a skin disease called mange. Mange causes animals to lose their hair and may turn their skin a blueish color.

SPOOKED!

Some people suggest the Chupacabra could be a wild dog infected with mange that attacks farm animals because the disease leaves it too weak to chase and catch wild prey.

WILD BEASTS

Hairy, Scary Creatures

Some of the scariest, hairiest creatures that spook us are those that look like humans. Reports of such creatures as Bigfoot in North America and the Yeti in the Himalayas in Asia tell of a large, hairy figure, like a man but different, looming out of the wilderness. Legends of a wild man like this are found in many cultures. Are they monsters that straddle the worlds of the human and the animal? Or perhaps they are animals, such as bears, that people mistake for monsters?

Beastly Bigfoot

The legendary Bigfoot is a large, hairy creature that roams the wild forests of North America and western Canada. It has been talked about for centuries and goes by many different names, including Sasquatch, Tree Man, and others. Reports of Bigfoot suggest it is 6 to 15 feet (1.8 to 4.5 m) tall and walks on two legs like a human. It smells awful and either moves eerily quietly or sometimes makes a **high-pitched** cry. Most scientists do not think Bigfoot exists but some people think that Bigfoot could be real. They say it could be the missing link, an animal midway in **evolution** between apes and humans.

A Mountain Monster

The Yeti is a wild, manly figure that lurks high up in the cold, snowy Himalaya Mountains. This huge, hairy beast is also known as the Abominable Snowman. It is said to be a cross between an ape and a bear, with enormous feet. Some say the footprints that are supposed to be from the Yeti were more likely to have been made by a bear. Bears sometimes walk in such a way that their front and back paws overlap, leaving what looks like an extra large human footprint.

Could the Yeti Be Real?

Some of the sightings and evidence people claim to be of the Yeti are believed to be hoaxes, or tricks. However, a professor from Oxford University in the UK examined some strands of hair said to be from the beast. He compared the **DNA** in the hairs to the DNA of a polar bear jawbone found in the Norwegian Arctic that was more than 40,000 years old. The professor said that similarities between the two suggest that there could be Yeti-like bears living in the Himalaya Mountains that have not been seen since the end of the last **Ice Age**!

While many people think the yeti is just a legend, there are those who believe it is a real human-like creature that lives in Nepal and China.

CHAPTER 4

CREATURES OF THE DEEP

Long before ships had radios, **GPS**, and other equipment to keep them safe, sailors put their lives at risk every time they left dry land. Sailing ships could be sunk by storms and rough waves, or **currents** could carry them off course and send them crashing into rocks. The deep, dark waters of the ocean remain mostly unknown to us but long ago, people knew so little about the creatures living in the deep that it is little wonder they feared mighty sea monsters.

Sea Monsters of the Past

Ancient maps of the oceans often included pictures of sea monsters, but these were not just illustrations. They were placed in unexplored areas of the oceans to warn sailors of the risks in these unknown waters. At the time, they were meant to be accurate depictions of what was believed to live in the sea. Sea monsters often turned out to be less terrifying than they seemed. Some were simply the rotting bodies of dead basking sharks and even huge clumps of seaweed.

The Killer Kraken

The kraken is an enormous, legendary sea monster that was said to be able to swallow an entire ship's crew in a single mouthful! It was said to capture an unsuspecting ship in its long, snakelike arms and crush it using a sharp, parrot-like beak. People think that this amazing creature may have been inspired by giant squid. These eight-armed sea creatures are enormous and have the largest eyes of any living creature.

Stories of ancient sea serpents and monsters came from sailors' fears of what lay in wait in the dark depths of the oceans.

Was the kraken monster really a giant squid, with its menacing eyes as large as a human head?

SPOOKED!

Unexplored areas in the waters on ancient maps of the sea were marked with a message such as "here there be dragons" and often an illustration of sea serpents or sea dragons. These monsters could in fact be pictures of the very real giant oarfish. This eel-shaped fish grows up to 30 feet (9 m) long and has a creepy crest of blood-red spines running down its head and back. It is also capable of swimming like a snake on the surface of the water.

A Japanese Sea Demon

The name Ushi-Oni translates to "ox demon," and this sea monster has the head of an ox and the body of a giant spider or crab. It is sometimes pictured with crablike claws, a long tail, and sharp horns. This massive sea monster mostly lives near water and is known for attacking and scaring people as they walk along a beach. It has powerful jaws with sharp fangs that can crush the hardest of objects. This beastly creature is also said to be able to release poison from its mouth.

The Umibōzu

The Umibōzu is a mythical Japanese sea creature that is said to live in the ocean. It appears to sailors on quiet nights when the water is calm. Suddenly, without any warning, a storm appears bringing high winds and rough waves. Then, the Umibōzu looms out of the depths, smashing the ship in a single blow or pulling it down to its doom in the deep.

The Bunyip

There are strange and spooky creatures living in other bodies of water, too. In **Aboriginal** Australian legends, the bunyip is a monster that lives in swamps and lagoons. It has flippers with long claws at the ends, a long neck, and a round body rather like a manatee or hippopotamus. The bunyip is said to have made booming or roaring noises as it ate humans. Stories of this creature may have started because of seals that rarely, but sometimes, swim upstream into the swamps and lagoons. The noise that people hear is likely to be a bittern, a bird that lives in marshland.

Mother of Water

Yacumama means "Mother of water" and the Yacumama is believed to be the mother of all creatures of the water, and even of the water itself. This monster lives in rivers in the Amazon rain forest in Peru. It takes the form of a giant snake and is said to be able to suck up any prey that comes close to it. The Yacumama legend is believed to come from sightings of a large snake such as a green anaconda, which can grow to 33 feet (10 m) long.

SPOOKED!

The Ushi-Oni has also been closely linked to illness so it may be that people imagined it to explain the unknown diseases that killed their loved ones.

Legend says that the bunyip prowled the land at night, in search of women and children to eat.

SEA CREATURES

Spooky Sea People

Centuries ago, when European sailors set out to explore the world, they returned with stories about mermaids or mermen they claim to have seen in the waves. The idea of these strange half-human, half-fish creatures soon spread around the world.

The Making of the Merpeople

In European legends, mermaids and mermen were natural beings that had magical powers. They loved music and often sang. Although they sometimes used their powers for good, and are often pictured combing their hair while balanced on a sea rock, they could be dangerous to people. If sailors angered them, merpeople could cause floods or other disasters. Long ago, sailors believed that if any of the crew saw a mermaid while on the water, their ship would likely be wrecked and sunk.

Mami Wata

Mermaid myths are told all around the world. In Africa, the water spirit Mami Wata (Mother Water) is often portrayed as a long haired, beautiful mermaid, half human and half fish. She can charm water snakes and she can be very dangerous. Mami Wata is known for kidnapping people while they are swimming or fishing. She takes them to her underwater spiritual world.

Song of the Sirens

Sirens are like sinister mermaids, except these mythical sea creatures are women with large feathers and birdlike feet, or they have the body of a bird and the head of a woman. Sirens are considered to be evil beings that live near the surface of the water and sing to sailors. Their **captivating** songs put sailors into a trance, and when they follow the song, their ships crash into the shore and sink.

Sailors Seeing Things

As stories of merpeople crossed the seas, more sailors saw what they thought were these sea creatures. But, people can see things they want to believe are true. Sometimes, these "mermaids" were actually sea mammals called manatees. Manatees have long, flat tails, which can make them look like mermaids.

Men or Manatees?

Christopher Columbus was a famous explorer who traveled the world. He was worried about meeting sea monsters on his voyages. When sailing close to Haiti in 1493, he reported seeing three mermaids who were "not as pretty as they are depicted, for somehow in the face they look like men." We now think that what Columbus saw were manatees!

In murky water, the way a manatee turns its head, the fingerlike bones in its front legs, and its flat tail might have fooled sailors into thinking it was a mermaid.

CHAPTER 5

MONSTERS FROM THE PAST

W e know that some of the scariest creatures ever to walk Earth existed because we have found their remains. These terrifying creatures include giant sharks like megalodon, super crocodiles, and saber-toothed tigers. Our planet must have been a fearful place. Some of the strange and scary creatures that people report seeing have not been proven to exist, yet... Could they be connected to the prehistoric monsters of the long-distant past?

Scary Then, Scary Now!

We already know that some of the real, ancient monsters still have relatives here on Earth. For example, Deinosuchus was a prehistoric alligator that even scared the mighty Tyrannosaurus rex dinosaurs! Deinosuchus was twice as heavy as the largest tyrannosaurs and as long as a big school bus. It roamed ancient swamps in what is now Mexico and the United States, catching sea turtles, dinosaurs, and other prey in its huge, blunt, and heavy teeth, which were the size of bananas. The American alligators of today are also huge. These giants are twice as long and four times as heavy as an average person.

Megalodon was the biggest fish ever known!

The Siberian unicorn was
a real animal!

SPOOKED!

The prehistoric
Siberian unicorn could
run quickly even though
it was so big, but there is
no proof that it could fly
like a mythical unicorn.

Unusual Unicorns

Greek travelers first told stories of
a one-horned magical unicorn more
than 2,000 years ago. Then, during
the Middle Ages, European sailors
sold long, white, spiral unicorn horns
to people who believed their magical
powers could cure illnesses. In fact,
these were tusks from the narwhal,
a beautiful whale that is also known
as the unicorn of the sea.

A Prehistoric Unicorn?

Archeologists have found **fossils** of
a Siberian unicorn that once walked
Earth alongside humans. The unicorn
was 13 feet (4 m) long and covered

in hair. It took its nickname
from the huge single horn on its
forehead. This unicorn was more
closely related to modern-day
rhinoceroses than horses. It is
believed the animal lived in what
is now Kazakhstan in Asia, before
it became **extinct**. Scientists are
trying to discover more about the
creature and why it died out.

The One Who Stops Rivers

In a remote area of central Africa, locals speak of a monster they see as "mokele-mbembe"—the "one who stops the flow of rivers"—because it is so large. Many people in the Democratic Republic of the Congo (DRC) have reported seeing a huge, strange animal living in deep swamps and lakes in the rain forest. They say it is brown and gray, the size of an elephant, with a long tail and a long neck. It uses its very long neck to pluck leaves and fruit from plants near the water's edge. It doesn't look like any other animal known to be alive on Earth today.

Some people think that the Loch Ness monster could be an animal that is similar to a prehistoric sea creature.

A Living Dinosaur?

Scientific expeditions to find the mokele-mbembe haven't found evidence yet, but does that mean it is not real? It is difficult for scientists to work in the remote and dense rain forests of the Congo, where venomous snakes and disease are common. However, the description of this mystery beast sounds much like a sauropod dinosaur. Sauropods were plant-eating dinosaurs with long necks and were the largest dinosaurs that ever lived. Could the legendary mokele-mbembe be a **descendant**?

The Loch Ness Monster

There is no clear evidence that the Loch Ness monster exists but there have been more than 1,100 recorded sightings of this beast. Many people believe that Nessie lives in a large lake called Loch Ness in Scotland. Loch Ness reaches incredible depths of 788 feet (240 m), so it is not difficult to imagine that something could be hiding in the deep water.

A Present-Day Plesiosaur?

Some people who claim to have seen Nessie describe it as an enormous animal, like a dragon or prehistoric monster. Many think that it looks similar to a plesiosaur, a sea reptile that lived millions of years ago. Some people believe that the Loch Ness monster is an ancient type of large animal that is yet to be identified.

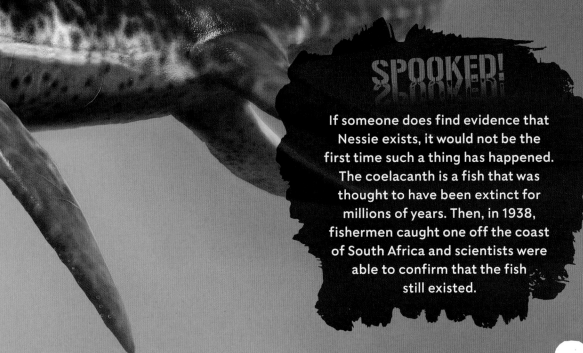

SPOOKED!

If someone does find evidence that Nessie exists, it would not be the first time such a thing has happened. The coelacanth is a fish that was thought to have been extinct for millions of years. Then, in 1938, fishermen caught one off the coast of South Africa and scientists were able to confirm that the fish still existed.

Dare to See Dragons?

The earliest stories of dragons date back thousands of years and these menacing monsters still haunt our imagination today. In Asian legends, dragons can be so small that they fit in a teacup but they can also be so big that they block out the Sun in the sky. They are said to be able to breathe clouds, change the seasons, and control rivers, lakes, and seas. In Europe, dragons are powerful and dangerous. They can kill people with their stinking breath and spit fire so hot it can set cities on fire. Some of these mythical dragons nest in caves, guard treasure, and feed on sheep or even people.

Dragon or Dinosaur?

Dragons are often described as enormous, reptile-like, and with threatening teeth and claws. Some people say this suggests that dragons might be descendants of Tyrannosaurus rex. These mighty dinosaurs died out long before humans walked on Earth, but people have mistaken their fossils for dragon bones.

SPOOKED!

Tyrannosaurus rex was one of the most ferocious **predators** that ever lived. It had a huge body, sharp teeth, and the strongest bite of any land animal, ever. Its jaws were so powerful they could crush a car!

Did fossil remains of the terrifying Tyrannosaurus rex spark old dragon stories?

The griffin was a scary combination of two powerful creatures.

The History of Griffins

Long ago, tales were told of a strange and scary creature with the head and wings of an eagle and the body of a lion. This creature was the griffin. The lion was considered to be the king of the beasts, while an eagle was the king of the birds. As a combination of these two, the griffin was feared as a very powerful beast and ruler of all creatures. The Roman author Pliny the Elder wrote that "griffins were said to lay eggs in burrows on the ground and these nests contained gold nuggets."

Grounds for the Griffin?

The remains of protoceratops dinosaurs, which lived around 80 million years ago, may have started rumors about griffins. It is thought that people digging for gold in the red sands of the Gobi Desert in Asia 5,000 years ago might have seen the remains of protoceratops dinosaurs. Protoceratops had a birdlike beak and a body with four legs, which is an unusual combination in the animal world. Protoceratops also had very long shoulder-blades, which may help to explain why griffins were said to have wings.

HUGE GIANTS

Tormenting Beasts

Giants are enormous and powerful creatures that look like very large human beings. Giants torment people in myths and folk tales from all over the world. Some of these mythical giants were only a few feet taller than an average human but others towered over the land like mountains. Some giants are gentle and kind while others are bad tempered and evil. Then there are those who can be a bit of both. Some have supernatural powers that they use in brutal and cruel ways.

Ancient Greek Giants

Many stories of giants were told by the ancient Greeks who believed they found bones of giants in the ground. Today, we suspect that the ancient Greeks were actually finding the enormous bones of large prehistoric creatures such as mammoths and woolly rhinoceroses, which once lived in the area. Over time, the skulls of prehistoric animals are crushed or broken up. This would leave only long bones, such as ribs and backbones, which are similar to human bones. That may have made the ancient Greeks believe they came from humanlike giants.

One-Eyed Giants

In Greek mythology, Cyclops are enormous giants with a single eye in the middle of their foreheads. These one-eyed giants are usually said to live on the island of Sicily in the Mediterranean Sea. Prehistoric elephants lived on this island long ago and fossils of their enormous skulls and bones can still be found in cliffs and hills there today. Many people believe that ancient Greeks may have mistaken the large hole in the center of the skull where the trunk was once attached for an enormous, single eye socket!

Antaeus the Giant

Long ago, the city of Tangiers in Morocco, Africa, was called Tingis. The people of Tingis claimed that a giant named Antaeus had built their city and that he was buried in a mound nearby. Roman soldiers did not believe the tale, so they dug into the mound in 81 BCE. They were amazed to find an enormous skeleton about 85 feet (26 m) long inside. Impressed, they reburied the remains with great honors. Modern scientists confirm that ancient elephant fossils are common in the area.

The ancient Greeks thought that the big mammoth bones they found were not human, and the enormous skeletons belonged to fearsome giants.

CHAPTER 6

FAKES AND HOAXES

Throughout history and across the world, people have been fascinated by tales of giants and other strange and scary creatures. Reports and sightings of such beasts bring even more excitement. Unfortunately, some of the evidence people have brought forward to show that they have seen such beasts, has been proven to be fakes and hoaxes, or tricks that deceive people into believing something that is not true.

Not the Loch Ness Monster!

In 1934, a photograph of what looks like the slender neck of a strange animal looming out of Loch Ness appeared in a UK newspaper. The photograph seemed to be firm evidence that Nessie actually exists. One reason the photo seemed so convincing was that it came from a London doctor named R. Kenneth Wilson. Few believed that such a respected doctor would lie. It wasn't until 60 years later, in 1994, that the photograph was proven to be a fake. Friends of Dr. Wilson had created a model of the monster out of a toy submarine and putty.

Today, people often mistake branches that rise up from the waters of Loch Ness for Nessie!

Barnum's fake mermaid
fooled many!

Making a Mermaid

In 1842, P.J. Barnum, the founder of Barnum's Circus and Barnum's American Museum, persuaded several US newspapers to publish articles about the remains of a mermaid he had on display in his museum. It was known as the Fiji Mermaid, because the sea captain who sold it to him had supposedly caught the mermaid near the Fiji Islands in the South Pacific Ocean. For many years, people were fooled into believing that the creepy exhibit was a real mermaid. Later, the so-called mermaid was revealed to really be a skeleton of a fish with the skeleton of a monkey's head sewn onto it.

SPOOKED!

In the nineteenth century, scientists became a bit bored of people trying to fool them with fakes and hoaxes. They became suspicious of people trying to trick them with bodies made up of parts of different animals attached together. So, when an animal with a furry body, a duck's bill, an otter's feet, and a tail like a beaver was given to scientists at the British Museum in the UK, some dismissed it as a prank. In fact, it was the Australian animal we know as the duck-billed platypus.

39

TALLER THAN GOLIATH

FEET 4 1/2 INCHES TALL

SIX MILLION PEOPLE HAVE PAID TO SEE HIM. D

P. T. BARNUM OFFERED $15

MOST VALUABLE SINGLE EXH

When the Cardiff Giant's tomb (see below) was opened for viewing, thousands of people came to see what some religious teachers were calling a giant that had perished in a flood that is written about in the Bible.

The Cardiff Giant was said to have fooled the whole nation when it was revealed in the United States many years ago.

The Case of the Cardiff Giant

In 1869, the people of Cardiff, New York, were stunned to learn that a giant had been discovered under the ground nearby. The story was that the 10-foot (3 m) figure had been turned to stone in the earth. People flocked from miles around to see the spectacle for themselves. A lot of Christian people in the area wanted to believe that the giant was real because a version of the Bible said that giantlike people had once lived on Earth.

Creating a Fake

Finally, it was proven that a man named George Hull had paid for a huge statue of a giant to be made. He had it secretly shipped to the village of Cardiff and buried in a pit. He got the idea after being surprised by a priest who believed giants once walked on Earth. A year later, he ordered two workmen to dig a well on that spot so they could make the surprising discovery. That didn't stop people from coming to see the "giant" or believing it was the real thing, and Hull made a lot of money from his hoax.

Giants have been the subjects of myths and legends throughout history.

Big Lies

There were other fake giants too. In 1958, there were reports of people seeing some enormous footprints in northern California. They were so big that many people started to think they could only have been made by a giant. Some scientists looked into the case to see if it was real. Some even thought it could be the missing link between **Neanderthals** and humans. The mystery continued until after the death of a man named Ray Wallace in 2002. His children then revealed that their father had made the gigantic footprints himself using a pair of feet he had carved from wood.

The Minnesota Iceman

In the 1960s, a man named Frank D. Hansen transported the body of a large, hairy humanlike creature he claimed could be Bigfoot around the United States. People queued up to see the 6-foot- (1.8 m) tall, hairy Minnesota Iceman, so-called because it was stored in ice. Hansen's traveling exhibition was a big hit. He told different stories about where it had come from, including one that a Japanese whaling ship found the body. It was later proven to be a fake made of latex rubber and hair.

A Tasmanian Mock Walrus?

On April 1 1984, the Orlando Sentinel newspaper reported on a strange new creature called the Tasmanian mock walrus. This beast was said to look like a walrus but it was only about 4 inches (10 cm) long. It was reported to be the "perfect pet" because it never needed bathing, used a litter box, and ate cockroaches. It was even supposed to purr like a cat! In fact, the picture showed a naked mole rat and the story was a joke for April Fool's Day!

Snowball the Giant Cat

In early 2000, a photo of an enormous white cat being held by a smiling bearded man appeared on the Internet and soon went viral. The cat was supposed to be called Snowball and it looked as big as a large dog. A caption claimed the man had found Snowball's average-sized mother wandering near a laboratory in Canada. He said that after Snowball was born she didn't stop growing. Finally, a man named Cordell Hauglie admitted he'd made the photo as a joke for friends.

Naked mole rats are pink, almost-hairless rodents that live in underground burrows in eastern Africa.

The description of the so-called thunderbird (see below) was similar to that of a prehistoric pterodactyl. Pterodactyls were giant flying reptiles that lived at the time of the dinosaurs.

Was the Tombstone thunderbird based on descriptions of a pterodactyl?

The Tombstone Thunderbird

In April 1890, a newspaper in the town of Tombstone, Arizona reported that a strange winged monster had been discovered and killed in the desert. The newspaper article said two cowboys spotted a giant birdlike creature with an enormous **wingspan** and chased the creature for several miles before shooting it. The creature was said to have had smooth skin, featherless wings, a head like an alligator's, and eyes as big as dinner plates. The report said the cowboys dragged the dead beast, known as a thunderbird, back to the town behind their horses.

Legend or Lie?

There were no more articles about the beast and no other evidence that the mysterious creature was actually brought back to Tombstone. Some say that the report was wildly exaggerated by the reporters or the two cowboys, which may have seen a large flying animal of some sort. One thing seems certain, either the newspaper or the cowboys were trying to spook the people of Tombstone into thinking prehistoric beasts were lurking nearby.

MAGICAL FAIRIES

Fairies Are Real?

Stories of the magical beings we call fairies have been around for thousands of years. Through the ages there have been descriptions of fairies as small elf-like creatures in green clothes or as tiny beings that live under mushrooms. Some people believe that fairies are real and in the early twentieth century, there was even evidence that seemed to prove that fairies that looked like tiny women with wings really did exist.

Fairy Fever

After World War I (1914–1918) there was a rise in interest in stories about fairies that became known as Fairy Fever in the UK. Fairies were everywhere: in children's books and plays and in grown-up poetry and newspapers. It seemed that people wanted to hear about magic and mystery to escape the horrors of the war they had been through. As interest in the supernatural increased, a group called the Fairy Investigation Society was set up to investigate fairies. One of the society's famous members was the author Sir Arthur Conan Doyle, who wrote the Sherlock Holmes stories.

Famous Photos

Conan Doyle was a firm believer in the supernatural. In 1920, he wrote a magazine article stating his belief in fairies. The article was illustrated with photographs that seemed to show fairies dancing. The photographs became known as the Cottingley Fairy photographs. Conan Doyle was a famous and trusted author and that made the idea that the photos were real even more believable.

Evidence at Last?

The fairy photos had been taken in 1917 by two young cousins named Elsie Wright and Frances Griffiths. The girls took the photographs by a stream in their backyard, in Cottingley, in the UK. Elsie's father dismissed the fairy pictures as a trick but Elsie's mother was interested in the supernatural and believed they were real. She showed the photographs to other people and they eventually made their way to Doyle.

The Truth

After the photographs were published, the cousins insisted that they were real. They stuck to this story for years. Then, in the 1980s, when the cousins were elderly ladies, they admitted the photographs were hoaxes. The girls had faked the photographs using paper cut-out images of fairies, which they then photographed.

Below are the Cottingley Fairies. Perhaps if people really want to believe in fairies, they are more likely to think that fake images of the magical beings are real.

GLOSSARY

Aboriginal the first people to live in a country

afterlife life after death

archeologists people who study history through artifacts and remains

captivating fascinating and interesting

currents areas of air or water moving in one direction

descendant a person who is related to someone who lived long ago

DNA the substance in cells that carries unique information about living things

evolution the way living things gradually change and form new species over many generations

extinct died out completely

folk tales stories traditionally shared by being spoken out loud

fossils remains of living things preserved in stone

gourd a large fruit that has a hard shell and cannot be eaten

GPS short for global positioning system, a network of satellites that tell people where they are on Earth

harvest to collect things to eat

high-pitched describes a sound that is squeakier than usual

hypnotize put someone into a sleep-like state in which they do as they are told

Ice Age the time when Earth was covered in ice, 2.6 million to 11,700 years ago

internal organs body parts inside the body such as the heart

legends traditional stories

Middle Ages the period between the end of the Roman Empire in CE 476 and about CE 1500

mortar a small bowl in which ingredients are crushed or ground

Neanderthals a type of humans who lived on Earth until about 40,000 years ago and who are now extinct

pestle a tool used to crush or grind ingredients

pharaoh an ancient Egyptian king

predators animals that hunt and eat other animals

remote far away

riddles questions or statements that offer a puzzle to be solved

rituals ceremonies performed for religious reasons

Scandinavia a group of northern European countries that includes Denmark, Norway, Finland, and Sweden

sinister evil and threatening

species a set of plants or animals that are all alike and can breed with each other

stake a rod of wood or metal with a point at one end

voodoo a religion based on magic and witchcraft

whey the watery part of milk

wingspan the distance from the end of one wing to the end of the other wing

FIND OUT MORE

Books

Claybourne, Anna. *History's Mysteries: Legends and Lore.*
National Geographic Kids, 2019.

Novak, Sara. *The Genius Kid's Guide to Mythical Creatures.*
North Star Editions, 2023.

Ward, Marchella. *Beasts of the Ancient World: A Kids' Guide to Mythical Creatures, from the Sphinx to the Minotaur, Dragons to Baku.*
Dorling Kindersley, 2023.

Websites

Learn more about Greek mythical creatures at
https://greekgodsandgoddesses.net/creatures

Find out about some more scary creatures at
https://facts.net/mythical-creatures

There is a world of mythical creatures at
www.newworldencyclopedia.org/entry/Mythical_creature

Publisher's note to educators and parents:
All the websites featured above have been carefully reviewed to ensure that they are suitable for students. However, many websites change often, and we cannot guarantee that a site's future contents will continue to meet our high standards of educational value. Please be advised that students should be closely monitored whenever they access the Internet.

INDEX

About the Author

Louise Spilsbury is an award-winning children's book author. She has written countless books about history and science. In writing and researching this book, she is more spooked than ever by strange and scary creatures!